Weekday Survival Cookbook

Over 100 Recipes & Tips to Survive a Busy Week

*When you see this symbol, you can be sure
the recipes have been well thought out
and thoroughly tested in <u>real kitchens</u> just like yours.
Like sharing a good recipe with friends,
we in the Kraft Creative Kitchens are pleased
to pass along our good food ideas to you.*

Weekday Survival Cookbook

Credits:

Director, Kraft Creative Kitchens
Marilyn Kruse
Manager, Kraft Creative Kitchens
Marjorie Fitch–Hilgenberg

Managing Editor
Jill Hidding
Editorial Associate
Tracy Patun

Recipe Development
**Jill Hidding, Tracy Patun,
Kay Lindsay, Jeanne Verlotta,
Jeannine Prentice**

Food Stylists
**Kimberley Loughlin, Janice Bell,
Patricia Nagle**

Photographers
**Jose Pascual, John Polich,
Joe Glyda, Tom Firak**

Prop Stylist
Cindy Neberz

Editorial
McDowell & Piasecki,Chicago, IL

Creative & Concept Development
**Marketing Corporation of America,
Westport, CT**

Design & Art Direction
Michael S. Cronin

Division Manager, Kraft Consumer
Promotion
Ron Toyama
Manager, Kraft Consumer Promotion
Eva Fitz
Associate Manager, Kraft Consumer
Promotion
Candy Lund
Project Supervisor, Kraft Consumer
Promotion
Maureen Becker

He l p!

If the clock striking six has you singing the "what's for dinner blues," you're not alone. After a hectic day, getting a meal on the table that's delicious and well-balanced is a challenge. That's what this book from the Kraft Creative Kitchens is all about.

The goal is to help you get through the work week–to help you plan, prepare and serve a terrific meal the whole family will love. Impossible you say?
Just wait.

Quick Recipes To **Survive** *A Busy Week.*

Start with a Game Plan!

The secret to weeknight cooking is planning.

✓ **Plan** menus for an entire week. You'll only need to make one trip to the market, and you won't be faced with any dinner decisions at 6:00 p.m.
– **Consider** flavor, texture, color and temperature.
– **Consider** good nutrition.
✓ **Plan** a two-course meal... a meat and vegetable main dish with a salad, or skip the salad and serve fresh fruit.
✓ **Plan** to use convenience foods paired with fresh ingredients.
✓ **Plan** to use "planned overs"...the extra chicken breasts or pork chops you cooked on Tuesday in Wednesday's fajitas.
✓ **Plan** to round out the menu with a purchased accompaniment... bakery bread, ice cream and cookies.
✓ **Plan** a well-stocked pantry, refrigerator and freezer.
– **Don't forget** *variety* when selecting staples.

> **TIP: Start with a macaroni and cheese dinner and add cooked chicken, green chilies, cherry tomato halves and and a dash of ground cumin for a fast skillet dish.**

- **Shop from a list**, adding just the ingredients you need to supplement what you have on hand.

✓**Plan** to purchase ingredients in the form in which you will use them...shredded cheese, boneless chicken breasts, chopped nuts, graham cracker crumbs.

PANTRY EXTENDERS
▼

Salsa/Picante sauce
Taco shells
Green/ripe olives
Sesame oil
Refried beans
Kidney beans
Pinto beans
Chow mein noodles
Water chestnuts
Flavored vinegars
Salad dressings (several flavors)
Dijon mustard
Canned whole tomatoes
Tomato paste
Pastas (several varieties)
White and brown rice (quick cooking)
Assorted nuts
Assorted crackers
Bagel/pita chips
Chocolate chips
Marshmallows
Brownie mix
Cake mix
Gelatin (assorted flavors)
Instant puddings (assorted flavors)
Caramels

TIP: Keep several shapes of dry pasta on hand. Freeze English muffins, tortillas and pitas as well as wheat, rye and French breads. Stock several different prepared salad dressings, ice cream toppings and cheese. A stash of frozen vegetables can be turned into fast side dishes or used as ingredients in salads and main dishes.

✓**Plan** to have the entire family pitch in. Divide the meal into parts and give *everyone* a job.

REFRIGERATOR/FREEZER EXTENDERS
▼

Italian sausage
Chorizo
Boneless chicken breasts
Ground turkey
Frozen cooked shrimp
Refrigerated pie crusts
Frozen fruits (assorted)
Frozen vegetables (assorted)
Ice cream
Frozen pound cake
Variety of breads/rolls
Variety of cheeses (natural, process)
Sour cream
Plain and flavored yogurt
Iceberg lettuce
Fresh fruit

Surviving the worst hour of the day.

The house is a mess, the phone is ringing, the stereo is blaring, and everyone's starving. Welcome home!

You're not alone. The same scene is being played out in homes all over the country. Why? According to family psychologists, the worst hour of the day happens because your children love and miss you during the workday. They know that home is a place where they can get rid of stress–where someone who loves them will listen and care.

Some tips for making homecoming more enjoyable...

...Give yourself 5 minutes before walking in the door to separate yourself from the office. Walk around the block or sit in the car with the radio on and your eyes closed.
...Spend the first 15 minutes at home paying attention to your family. Share a small, nutritious snack. Then play a game, read a story or listen to a tape together.
...Set aside one activity that your kids really enjoy for your arrival home. While you start dinner, they'll be happy and busy with modeling clay or a video game.
...Encourage everyone to help with dinner. Kids like to feel needed. Let them fill water glasses with ice, wash vegetables, butter bread, scoop ice cream and fold napkins.

Make Dinner an Event!

For many families, dinner is the only meal eaten together. A few "house rules" can turn the dinner hour into a family hour that will help everyone recharge and reconnect after a hectic day.

"House Rules"

1. Make the television set off limits. Ditto for newspapers, books and magazines.
2. Save heavy discussions (report cards, the family budget, misbehavior) for another time.
3. Share the highlights of the day–an "A" on a spelling test, a soccer game win, a promotion, a class field trip.
4. Let everyone have a chance to share in the table conversation.
5. Talk about current events, a movie you just saw or last night's ballgame.
6. Occasionally add flowers or candles to the table.

Cook something New!

Kraft Weekday Survival Cookbook is an idea book. Divided into four main sections–*The Main Event, Super Side Dishes, Sweets and Treats,* and *Spur of the Moment Entertaining*– it offers dozens of ideas for easy, delicious weeknight menus.

• Burgers and toppers, pizzas for *every* taste, sandwiches, hearty main dish soups and microwave entrees. They're all in The Main Event.

• Salads, stir-in ideas for pastas and rice and jazzed-up veggies are Super Side Dishes that round out the main event.

• End the meal on a sweet note–or satisfy a snack attack–with an *Outrageous Brownie* or *Caramelcorn* from Sweets and Treats.

• Unexpected guests? In Spur of the Moment Entertaining, look for an assortment of fix-it-fast snacks, appetizers and dips–many with just 3 or 4 ingredients.

Ready, set, get planning!

◄ Problem:

Where's Mom?
I'm starved...
When can we eat?

▲ Solution:

Delegate! Give everyone a job. Ask older kids to make a
dessert while the younger ones tear lettuce for a salad
or set the table. A make-ahead main dish on the menu?
The first one home pops it into the oven or microwave.

The

Main

Event

Center of the plate gets a new look—flavorful main dishes that take minutes to prepare or can be made ahead and baked or microwaved just before serving. Sandwiches, burgers and pizza are fun fast food. Craving a favorite ethnic flavor? Savor pastas, fajitas, enchiladas and calzones. Our recipe for Barbecue Meatloaf cooks in just 14 minutes in the microwave and tastes like Mom's.

The Convenient Cut– Boneless, Skinless Chicken Breast

Quick cooking and versatile boneless, skinless chicken breasts are the quick cook's staple. Use as fillets, pound into "cutlets," cut into strips for stir-frys or cubes for soups and casseroles.

Pecan Chicken

Helpful Hints

✓ Boneless, skinless chicken breast halves usually are sold four per package.

✓ Stock up when chicken breasts are on sale; freeze in recipe-size portions.

✓ Chicken cutlets – boneless, skinless breasts pounded to ¼-inch thickness between two sheets of plastic wrap – cook in 4 to 6 minutes.

✓ Check for doneness. When cooked, chicken breasts should be tender and no longer pink in the center.

Pecan Chicken (opposite)

Prep time: 10 minutes plus marinating
Cooking time: 12 minutes
Oven-fried cooking time: 20 minutes

4	(approx. 1¼ lbs.) boneless, skinless chicken breasts
½	cup *SEVEN SEAS VIVA CREAMY ITALIAN! Dressing*
½	cup fresh bread crumbs
½	cup finely chopped pecans
¼	cup *PARKAY Margarine*

▶ Place chicken in shallow dish or plastic bag.

▶ Pour dressing over chicken. Cover; marinate in refrigerator 1 to 8 hours. Drain.

▶ Dip chicken in combined crumbs and pecans; press to coat.

▶ Cook chicken in margarine in large skillet over medium heat 5 to 6 minutes on each side or until tender.   4 servings

Oven-Fried Method:

▶ Preheat oven to 375°.

▶ Place breaded chicken in shallow baking dish or jelly roll pan. Drizzle melted margarine over chicken.

▶ Bake 15 to 20 minutes or until chicken is tender.

Chicken Fajitas

Prep time: 20 minutes
Cooking time: 15 minutes

4	(approx. 1¼ lbs.) boneless, skinless chicken breasts, cut into thin strips
3	tablespoons oil
1	green pepper, cut into strips
1	red pepper, cut into strips
1	small onion, sliced
2	garlic cloves, minced
1	(8 oz.) container *PHILADELPHIA BRAND Soft Cream Cheese with Herb & Garlic*
16	(6-inch) flour tortillas, warmed

▶ Saute half of chicken in 1 tablespoon oil in large skillet until tender; remove from skillet. Repeat with 1 tablespoon oil and remaining chicken.

▶ Saute peppers, onions and garlic in remaining 1 tablespoon oil until crisp-tender. Add chicken to skillet; mix well.

▶ Spread approximately 1 tablespoon cream cheese over each tortilla. Place ½ cup chicken mixture in center of each tortilla; roll up. Serve with salsa, if desired.   8 servings

Quick Saucy Chicken Stir-Fry (below)

Prep time: 20 minutes
Cooking time: 10 minutes

3	tablespoons oil
1	cup broccoli flowerets
1	cup cauliflowerets
¾	cup 2-inch julienne-cut carrots
¼	cup green onion slices
1	garlic clove, minced
3	(approx. 1 lb.) boneless, skinless chicken breasts, cut into thin strips
½	cup *MIRACLE WHIP Salad Dressing*
1	tablespoon soy sauce
½	teaspoon ground ginger
½	teaspoon crushed red pepper flakes (optional) Hot cooked *MINUTE Premium Long Grain Rice*

▶ Heat 1 tablespoon oil in wok or large skillet over medium-high heat. Add vegetables and garlic; stir-fry 4 to 5 minutes or until crisp-tender. Remove vegetables from pan.

▶ Add remaining oil and chicken to pan; stir-fry 4 minutes or until tender.

▶ Reduce heat; stir in vegetables and remaining ingredients. Simmer 1 minute, stirring occasionally. Serve over hot cooked rice. Sprinkle with crushed red pepper flakes.   4 servings

Variations: Substitute *MIRACLE WHIP LIGHT Reduced Calorie Salad Dressing* for salad dressing.

Substitute ¾ lb. cleaned shrimp for chicken. Reduce final stir-frying time from 4 minutes to 2 to 3 minutes or until shrimp is pink.

Quick Saucy Chicken Stir-Fry

Pizza–Plain and Fancy

Everyone loves pizza! Joining the familiar sausage, mozzarella and crispy crust are new wave toppers and bottoms.

Pizza Your Way

Helpful Hints

✓ Try pairing two or three different cheeses – cheddar with mozzarella, parmesan with gouda.

✓ Substitute crumbled cooked chorizo or Polish sausage for the traditional Italian sausage.

✓ Round out a pizza supper with a green salad and fruit.

✓ Freeze leftover pizza by the slice for a fast snack.

Pizza Your Way (opposite)

Have fun with pizza and create your own special recipe! Pizza doesn't have to be Italian. Try a barbecue, Mexican, seafood or Hawaiian style. Here are some ideas to get you started:

▶ Start with a base of: refrigerated pizza crust, tortillas, pita bread, English muffins, bagels, French or Italian bread.

▶ Spread with: pizza sauce, tomato sauce and Italian herbs, salsa, barbecue sauce, chili, cocktail sauce, Italian dressing, cheese snack or soft herbed cream cheese.

▶ Top with: sausage, pepperoni, hamburger, bacon, ham or Canadian bacon, hot dogs, salmon, crab, shrimp, tuna, anchovies, chicken or turkey.

▶ Add: mushrooms, peppers, onions, green onions, olives, spinach, artichoke hearts, asparagus, avocados, tomato slices, chili peppers, roasted red peppers, pineapple, garlic, nuts, zucchini or yellow squash.

▶ Sprinkle with: mozzarella, cheddar, parmesan, provolone, gouda, monterey jack or Swiss cheese, crushed red pepper flakes, fresh or dried herbs.

Vegetarian Pizza
Prep time: 10 minutes
Cooking time: 20 minutes

1   **(12-inch) ready-made pizza crust**
3   **tablespoons olive oil**
1   **cup (4 ozs.) *100% Natural KRAFT Shredded Low-Moisture Part-Skim Mozzarella Cheese***
1   **cup (4 ozs.) *KRAFT 100% Grated Parmesan Cheese***
1   **cup mushroom slices**
1   **cup red onion slices**
1   **cup seeded chopped tomato**
1   **teaspoon Italian seasoning**
½   **teaspoon garlic powder**

▶ Preheat oven to 450°.

▶ Brush pizza crust with 1 tablespoon oil.

▶ Top with mozzarella cheese and ½ cup parmesan cheese.

▶ Saute mushrooms, onions, tomatoes and seasonings in 2 tablespoons oil until tender.

▶ Spoon over cheeses. Sprinkle with remaining parmesan cheese.

▶ Bake 20 minutes on bottom rack of oven.   6 servings

Variation: Saute one (8 oz.) pkg. *LOUIS KEMP Crab Delight Flakes* with vegetables. Continue as directed.

Chicken Fajita Pizzas (below)
Prep time: 10 minutes
Cooking time: 15 minutes

4   **(6-inch) flour tortillas**
1½   **cups (6 ozs.) *VELVEETA Mexican Shredded Pasteurized Process Cheese Food***
1   **cup shredded cooked chicken**
½   **cup salsa**
½   **cup chopped green pepper**
½   **cup seeded chopped tomato**
¼   **cup pitted ripe olive slices**

▶ Preheat oven to 350°.

▶ Place tortillas on cookie sheet; sprinkle 2 tablespoons process cheese food on each tortilla.

▶ Bake 4 to 5 minutes or until process cheese food is melted.

▶ Toss chicken with salsa; spread on tortillas.

▶ Top with remaining process cheese food.

▶ Bake 7 to 10 minutes or until thoroughly heated and process cheese food is melted.

▶ Top with remaining ingredients.   4 servings

Chicken Fajita Pizzas

Burgers and Toppers

Why settle for a plain burger when you can have it your way with the flavors you crave...Greek, Italian, Tex-Mex, Californian.

Clockwise from left: Special Burger Sauce, Cucumber Onion Sauce, Zippy Mustard Sauce

Helpful Hints

✓ For moist, juicy burgers, handle ground beef gently and as little as possible.

✓ Shape ground beef into patties. Freeze on cookie sheets until firm; transfer to resealable freezer bag. Frozen burgers can be broiled successfully if you increase the broiling time.

✓ Grill extra burgers for a second meal. Freeze with sheets of waxed paper between. Thaw on DEFROST, separating burgers, and removing waxed paper while partially frozen. Arrange in circle on microwave safe rack in baking dish to completely defrost and to reheat.

✓ Change the look by varying the bread. Try toasted slices of sourdough, a whole wheat pita or an English muffin half.

Special Burger Sauce (opposite)
Prep time: 5 minutes plus chilling

¾   **cup KRAFT LIGHT Cholesterol Free Reduced Calorie Mayonnaise**
3   **tablespoons dill pickle relish**
3   **tablespoons catsup**

▶ Mix together ingredients until well blended; chill.   1 cup

Cucumber Onion Sauce (opposite)
Prep time: 5 minutes plus chilling

¾   **cup KRAFT LIGHT Cholesterol Free Reduced Calorie Mayonnaise**
⅓   **cup seeded chopped cucumber**
2   **tablespoons chopped onion**

▶ Mix together ingredients until well blended; chill.   1 cup

Zippy Mustard Sauce (opposite)
Prep time: 5 minutes plus chilling

¾   **cup KRAFT LIGHT Cholesterol Free Reduced Calorie Mayonnaise**
2   **tablespoons KRAFT Pure Prepared Mustard**
2½   **teaspoons Worcestershire sauce**

▶ Mix together ingredients until well blended; chill.   ¾ cup

Cheesy Guacamole Topper
Prep time: 10 minutes

¼   **lb. VELVEETA Pasteurized Process Cheese Spread, cubed**
½   **cup sour cream**
2   **avocados, peeled, cut into 1-inch pieces**
1   **tomato, cut into 1-inch pieces**
½   **small onion, cut into 1-inch pieces**
1   **fresh jalapeño pepper, seeded, coarsely chopped**
1   **tablespoon lemon juice**
   Few drops hot pepper sauce

▶ Place ingredients in food processor container with steel blade attached; process until coarsely chopped.   3 cups

Garden Vegetable Cheese Topper
Prep time: 10 minutes

1   **(10.5 oz.) container SPREADERY Cheese Snack Neufchatel Cheese with Garden Vegetables**
½   **cup chopped zucchini**
½   **cup seeded chopped tomato**

▶ Mix together ingredients until well blended.   1 ¾ cups

Malibu Burger Topper
Prep time: 5 minutes plus chilling

¼   **cup KRAFT Real Mayonnaise**
¼   **cup sour cream**
¼   **cup finely chopped onion**
1   **tablespoon chopped parsley**

▶ Mix together ingredients until well blended; chill.   ¾ cup

Barbecued Hamburgers (below)
Prep time: 10 minutes
Cooking time: 10 minutes

1   **lb. ground beef**
½   **teaspoon salt**
¼   **teaspoon pepper**
½   **cup KRAFT Barbecue Sauce**

▶ Mix together meat, salt and pepper. Shape into four patties.

▶ Place on greased grill over hot coals (coals will be glowing).

▶ Grill, uncovered, 10 minutes or to desired doneness, turning and brushing with barbecue sauce.   4 servings

Variation: Substitute 1 lb. LOUIS RICH Ground Turkey for ground beef.

Barbecued Hamburgers

Microwave Gourmet

Celebrate straight A's, a birthday or promotion with a special dinner that's microwave quick. Fish, ground turkey and beef are naturals for microwave cooking.

Halibut Steaks with Dijon Sauce

Helpful Hints

✓ Fish is completely cooked when the flesh becomes opaque and it flakes easily with a fork.

✓ Haddock, orange roughy, sole, cod and swordfish are mild in flavor and can be substituted for halibut.

✓ Always check for doneness after minimum time stated in the recipe. Food will continue to cook a short time during standing. Remember to cover the dish during standing to retain heat.

✓ Use waxed paper or white paper towels to prevent splatters and to cover foods that might become soggy if tightly covered.

Halibut Steaks
with Dijon Sauce (opposite)

Prep time: 5 minutes
Microwave cooking time: 7 minutes

½   cup *SEVEN SEAS VIVA RANCH!* Dressing
1   tablespoon Dijon mustard
2   (1 to 1½-inch) halibut steaks

▶ Stir together dressing and mustard. Brush ¼ cup sauce on both sides of fish; reserve remaining sauce.

▶ Arrange fish in 8-inch square baking dish with thickest portions toward outside of dish. Cover with plastic wrap; vent.

▶ Microwave on HIGH 4 to 7 minutes, turning dish after 3 minutes. Let stand, covered, 2 to 3 minutes or until fish flakes easily with fork. Serve with remaining sauce.   4 servings

Midwestern Stir-Fry

Prep time: 10 minutes
Microwave cooking time: 7 minutes
Conventional cooking time: 10 minutes

½   cup *MIRACLE WHIP Salad Dressing*
2   tablespoons milk
½   teaspoon *KRAFT Pure Prepared Mustard*
½   lb. smoked sausage, cut into ¼-inch slices, halved
¾   cup yellow squash slices, halved
½   cup green or red pepper strips
½   cup 1-inch green onion slices
**   Hot cooked *MINUTE Premium Long Grain Rice***

▶ Mix together salad dressing, mustard and milk until well blended; set aside.

▶ Combine sausage, peppers and onions in medium bowl. Microwave on HIGH 2 minutes. Stir in squash. Continue microwaving on HIGH 2 minutes or until vegetables are crisp-tender.

▶ Add salad dressing mixture; mix lightly. Microwave on MEDIUM (50%) 2 to 3 minutes or until thoroughly heated, stirring after 2 minutes (do not overcook). Serve over rice. 4 servings

Conventional:

▶ Mix together salad dressing, mustard and milk until well blended; set aside.

▶ Stir-fry sausage in large skillet or wok until hot. Remove sausage from skillet; drain, reserving 1 tablespoon fat. Return fat to skillet.

▶ Add squash and peppers. Stir-fry 3 minutes.

▶ Return sausage to skillet with onions; stir-fry 1 minute. Remove from heat.

▶ Add salad dressing mixture; mix lightly. Serve over rice.

Barbecue Meatloaf (below)

Prep time: 10 minutes
Microwave cooking time: 14 minutes plus standing
Conventional cooking time: 50 minutes plus standing

1   lb. ground beef
½   cup *KRAFT THICK 'N SPICY Original Barbecue Sauce* or *KRAFT Barbecue Sauce*
½   cup old fashioned or quick oats, uncooked
½   cup finely chopped onion
1   egg, beaten

▶ Mix together all ingredients except ¼ cup barbecue sauce.

▶ Shape into loaf in 12 x 8-inch baking dish.

▶ Microwave on HIGH 12 to 14 minutes or until center is no longer pink, turning dish after 6 minutes. Let stand 5 minutes. Serve with remaining barbecue sauce.   4 servings

Conventional:

▶ Preheat oven to 375°.

▶ Mix together all ingredients except ¼ cup barbecue sauce.

▶ Shape into loaf in 12 x 8-inch baking dish.

▶ Bake 45 to 50 minutes or until center is no longer pink. Let stand 5 minutes. Serve with remaining barbecue sauce.

Variation: Substitute 1 lb. *LOUIS RICH Ground Turkey* for ground beef.

Barbecue Meatloaf, Cheesy Mashed Potatoes

Pasta Ready, Set, Go

Start with a box of pasta, add on-hand ingredients and serve a pasta sensation.

Pasta Plus

Pasta Plus (opposite)

Pasta can be more than noodles with tomato sauce. Open up your cupboards and refrigerator for new ideas or follow some of our suggestions:

▶ Stir into hot cooked pasta: *CHEEZ WHIZ Pasteurized Process Cheese Spread, PARKAY Margarine* and *KRAFT 100% Grated Parmesan Cheese, PHILADELPHIA BRAND Soft Flavored Cream Cheese, SPREADERY Cheese Snack* or *VELVEETA Pasteurized Process Cheese Spread.*

▶ Add: hot cooked vegetables, chopped cooked meat, poultry or seafood, fresh or dried herbs.

Spaghetti Parmesan

Conventional cooking time: 15 minutes
Microwave cooking time: 10 minutes

1	**(32 oz.) jar spaghetti sauce**
²/₃	**cup (3 ozs.) *KRAFT 100% Grated Parmesan Cheese***
1	**(16 oz.) pkg. spaghetti, cooked, drained**

▶ Heat sauce according to label directions.

▶ Stir in parmesan cheese; simmer 10 minutes, stirring occasionally.

▶ Pour sauce over spaghetti. Sprinkle with additional parmesan cheese.   6 servings

Microwave:

▶ Microwave sauce in 2-quart casserole or bowl on HIGH 4 minutes; stir in parmesan cheese.

▶ Microwave on HIGH 2 to 6 minutes or until thoroughly heated, stirring every 2 minutes.

▶ Pour sauce over spaghetti. Sprinkle with additional parmesan cheese.

Fettucini with Vegetable Sauce

Prep time: 10 minutes
Cooking time: 15 minutes

½	**cup chopped onion**
2	**medium zucchini, sliced**
2	**tablespoons *PARKAY Margarine***
1	**(10.5 oz.) container *SPREADERY Cheese Snack Neufchatel Cheese with Garlic & Herb***
½	**cup milk**
1	**cup seeded chopped tomato**
8	**ozs. fettucini, cooked, drained**

▶ Saute onion and zucchini in margarine until tender; reduce heat

▶ Add cheese snack and milk; stir until thoroughly heated.

▶ Add tomato.

▶ Serve sauce over hot fettucini.   4 to 6 servings

Kids Favorite Macaroni and Cheese

Prep time: 10 minutes
Cooking time: 7 minutes

1	**(8 oz.) jar *CHEEZ WHIZ Pasteurized Process Cheese Spread***
2	**cups (7 ozs.) elbow macaroni, cooked, drained**
4	***OSCAR MAYER Wieners*, cut into 1-inch pieces, heated**

▶ Heat process cheese spread according to label directions. Pour over macaroni and wieners; mix lightly.   4 servings

Variation: Add one (14 ¼ oz.) can stewed tomatoes, drained, cut up.

Parmesan Carbonara (below)

Prep/cooking time: 15 minutes

8	**ozs. linguine**
4	**eggs, beaten**
¼	**cup *PARKAY Margarine*, melted**
¼	**cup milk**
¾	**cup (3 ozs.) *KRAFT 100% Grated Parmesan Cheese***
4	***OSCAR MAYER Bacon Slices*, crisply cooked, crumbled**
¼	**cup chopped parsley**

▶ Cook linguine as directed on package. Drain; do not rinse.

▶ Return to pan; toss with eggs, margarine and milk.

▶ Add remaining ingredients; heat thoroughly, stirring occasionally. Serve with additional cheese, if desired. 4 to 6 servings

Parmesan Carbonara

Start With A KRAFT Dinner Or Side Dish

Cook's night off? Let the kids make dinner the easy, fun way with a packaged dinner or side dish.

Busy Day Turkey Divan

Helpful Hints

✓ Top wedges of iceberg lettuce with a pourable dressing for a fast salad.

✓ No shrimp? Substitute cooked chicken in *Creole Mac.*

✓ Give a new look to *Busy Day Turkey Divan* and *Macaroni Florentine* by serving in individual casseroles or au gratin dishes.

✓ Plan to serve *Mac 'N Cheese Primavera* early in the week, and buy precut vegetables at the supermarket salad bar to save chopping time.

Busy Day Turkey Divan (opposite)

Prep time: 15 minutes
Cooking time: 30 minutes

½	cup *KRAFT Real Mayonnaise*
2	tablespoons flour
¾	cup milk
1	(14 oz.) pkg. *KRAFT Deluxe Macaroni and Cheese Dinner*
1	(10 oz.) pkg. *BIRDS EYE Broccoli Spears*, thawed, drained
1	(6 oz.) pkg. *LOUIS RICH Oven Roasted Turkey Breast Slices*
2	tablespoons *KRAFT 100% Grated Parmesan Cheese*

▶ Preheat oven to 350°.

▶ Blend mayonnaise and flour in saucepan over low heat. Gradually add milk; cook, stirring constantly, until thickened.

▶ Prepare Dinner as directed on package.

▶ Spoon Dinner into 10 x 6-inch baking dish. Arrange broccoli spears and turkey slices over Dinner. Top with mayonnaise mixture; sprinkle with cheese.

▶ Bake 30 minutes or until thoroughly heated OR refrigerate overnight. When ready to serve, bake, covered, 30 to 35 minutes or until thoroughly heated.   6 servings

Macaroni Florentine

Prep time: 10 minutes
Cooking time: 15 minutes

1	(14 oz.) pkg. *KRAFT Deluxe Macaroni and Cheese Dinner*
1	cup mushroom slices
½	cup chopped onion
2	tablespoons *PARKAY Margarine*
1	(10 oz.) pkg. *BIRDS EYE Chopped Spinach*, thawed, well drained

▶ Prepare Dinner as directed on package.

▶ Saute mushrooms and onions in margarine until tender. Add to Dinner with spinach; mix lightly.   6 servings

Creole Mac (below)

Prep time: 10 minutes
Cooking time: 15 minutes

1	(14 oz.) pkg. *KRAFT Deluxe Macaroni and Cheese Dinner*
¼	cup chopped green pepper
¼	cup chopped onion
2	tablespoons *PARKAY Margarine*
1	(14 ½ oz.) can tomatoes, drained, cut up
½	lb. medium cooked shrimp
¼	to ½ teaspoon hot pepper sauce

▶ Prepare Dinner as directed on package.

▶ Saute green peppers and onions in margarine until crisp-tender.

▶ Add remaining ingredients; stir over medium heat until thoroughly heated.   6 servings

Creole Mac

Start With A
KRAFT Dinner Or Side Dish
(continued)

Mac 'N Cheese Primavera

Mac 'N Cheese Primavera (opposite)

Prep time: 15 minutes

1	(7 ¼ oz.) pkg. *KRAFT Macaroni and Cheese Dinner*
1	cup broccoli flowerets
1	cup zucchini slices
1	cup red or green pepper strips
2	tablespoons green onion slices
2	tablespoons *PARKAY Margarine*
¼	teaspoon dried oregano leaves, crushed

▶ Prepare Dinner as directed on package.

▶ Saute vegetables in margarine until crisp-tender. Add Dinner and oregano; mix lightly.   6 servings

Beef & Potatoes Stroganoff

Prep time: 10 minutes
Cooking time: 25 minutes

1	lb. beef sirloin, cut into thin strips
1	tablespoon oil
1	cup mushroom slices
½	cup chopped onion
1	(5.8 oz.) pkg. *KRAFT Scalloped Potatoes & Cheese*
½	cup sour cream
¼	cup chopped parsley

▶ Brown meat in oil; drain. Stir in mushrooms and onions; cook until tender. Remove from pan.

▶ In same pan, prepare Potatoes & Cheese as directed on package for stove top, except omitting margarine.

▶ Stir in remaining ingredients; cook until thoroughly heated. 4 servings

Skillet Chili Mac

Prep/cooking time: 20 minutes

½	lb. ground beef
1	(14 oz.) pkg. *KRAFT Deluxe Macaroni and Cheese Dinner*
2	cups water
1	(8 oz.) can tomato sauce
¼	cup chopped onion
¼	cup chopped green pepper
2	teaspoons chili powder

▶ Brown meat; drain. Add all remaining ingredients except Cheese Sauce; mix well.

▶ Bring to boil; reduce heat. Cover; simmer 8 to 10 minutes or until Macaroni is tender, stirring occasionally.

▶ Remove from heat. Stir in Cheese Sauce.   4 to 6 servings

Pork & Peppers Pasta (below)

Prep time: 10 minutes
Cooking time: 10 minutes

½	lb. lean pork, cut into thin strips
1	garlic clove, minced
2	tablespoons oil
1	(6.0 oz.) pkg. *KRAFT Cheddar Broccoli Pasta & Cheese*
1	red pepper, cut into strips
¼	cup green onion slices
2	tablespoons dry white wine (optional)

▶ Stir-fry pork and garlic in oil in 2-quart saucepan. Remove from pan.

▶ In same pan, prepare Pasta & Cheese as directed on package, except omitting margarine and adding pork and remaining ingredients during last 3 minutes of cooking. Remove from heat. Cover; let stand 2 minutes.   3 to 4 servings

Pork & Peppers Pasta

Make Ahead

Night 1: Assemble these family favorites over the weekend or the night before in their own baking dish and refrigerate.

Night 2: Pop the dish in the oven or microwave, toss together a salad and relax. You deserve it!

Spinach Lasagna

Helpful Hints

✓ Lightly spray casserole dish with nonstick cooking spray for easy cleanup.

✓ Freeze leftovers in small microwaveable containers to add to brown bag lunches.

✓ No mostaccioli on the shelf? Substitute rigatoni (tubes), rotini (spirals), penne (quills) or rotelle (wheels).

✓ For variety, substitute Italian sausage or ground turkey for beef in *Mostaccioli and Beef Bake*.

Spinach Lasagna (opposite)

Prep time: 20 minutes
Cooking time: 35 minutes plus standing

1	**(15 oz.) pkg. ricotta cheese**
1	**(10 oz.) pkg. _BIRDS EYE Chopped Spinach_, thawed, well drained**
½	**cup (2 ozs.) _KRAFT 100% Grated Parmesan Cheese_**
1	**egg**
3	**cups spaghetti sauce**
8	**ozs. lasagna noodles, cooked, drained**
1	**(16 oz.) pkg. _100% Natural KRAFT Low-Moisture Part-Skim Mozzarella Cheese Slices_**

▶ Preheat oven to 375°.

▶ Mix together ricotta cheese, spinach, parmesan cheese and egg until well blended.

▶ Layer 1 cup sauce, three noodles, 1 cup ricotta cheese mixture and three mozzarella cheese slices in 12 x 8-inch baking dish. Repeat layers twice. Cover with foil.

▶ Bake 20 minutes; remove foil and continue baking 15 minutes, OR refrigerate overnight. When ready to serve, bake, covered, 30 minutes; remove foil and continue baking 15 minutes. Let stand 10 minutes.   6 to 8 servings

Mostaccioli and Beef Bake

Prep time: 15 minutes
Cooking time: 25 minutes

2	**cups (5½ ozs.) mostaccioli, cooked, drained**
1	**lb. ground beef**
1	**(15½ oz.) jar spaghetti sauce**
½	**cup (2 ozs.) _KRAFT 100% Grated Parmesan Cheese_**
1	**cup _100% Natural KRAFT Shredded Low-Moisture Part-Skim Mozzarella Cheese_**

▶ Preheat oven to 350°.

▶ Brown meat; drain. In large mixing bowl, toss noodles with meat, sauce and parmesan cheese. Spoon into 12 x 8-inch baking dish. Top with mozzarella cheese; cover.

▶ Bake 25 minutes or until thoroughly heated OR refrigerate overnight. When ready to serve, bake, covered, 40 minutes or until thoroughly heated.   6 servings

Microwave:

▶ Prepare as directed above, except do not top with mozzarella cheese. Microwave on HIGH 7 to 8 minutes or until thoroughly heated, stirring after 4 minutes.

▶ Top with mozzarella cheese. Microwave on HIGH 2 minutes or until cheese is melted.

Tex-Mex Chicken Fiesta (below)

Prep time: 20 minutes
Cooking time: 20 minutes plus standing

1	**(10¾ oz.) can condensed cream of chicken soup**
¾	**cup cold water**
2	**teaspoons chili powder**
½	**teaspoon cumin**
2	**cups _MINUTE Rice_**
2	**cups chopped cooked chicken or turkey**
¼	**cup diced red pepper**
¼	**cup diced green pepper**
1	**cup (4 ozs.) shredded _CASINO Natural Monterey Jack Cheese_**
1	**cup (4 ozs.) shredded _100% Natural KRAFT Mild Cheddar Cheese_**

▶ Preheat oven to 350°.

▶ Mix together soup, water, chili powder and cumin. Cook 5 minutes over medium heat, stirring occasionally.

▶ Add all remaining ingredients except ½ cup each cheese.

▶ Spoon mixture into 10 x 6-inch baking dish.

▶ Top with remaining cheese. Bake 20 minutes or until thoroughly heated, OR cover; refrigerate overnight. When ready to serve, bake, uncovered, 40 to 45 minutes or until thoroughly heated. Let stand 5 minutes before serving. Top with sour cream, salsa and cilantro, if desired.   4 to 6 servings

Variation: Substitute _LOUIS RICH Oven Roasted Boneless Turkey Breast_ for cooked chicken or turkey.

Tex-Mex Chicken Fiesta

Planned Overs

Cook once, dine twice. When chicken is on the menu (or pork chops or steak), cook enough for two meals. Then, use the extras in a fast skillet dish, casserole, sandwich or salad a night or two later.

Turkey Enchiladas Con Queso

Helpful Hints

✓ Wrap and refrigerate planned overs promptly and use within 2 days.

✓ No planned overs? Use chicken or turkey breast, ham, roast beef or corned beef from the supermarket deli.

✓ To keep tortillas from cracking, microwave in stacks of four between damp white paper towels on HIGH 30 seconds to 1 minute.

✓ Keep dehydrated potato flakes on the shelf for mashed potatoes in an instant.

Turkey Enchiladas Con Queso (opposite)

Prep time: 15 minutes
Microwave cooking time: 20 minutes

1	cup chopped cooked turkey or chicken
1	(8 oz.) pkg. *PHILADELPHIA BRAND Cream Cheese*, softened
¼	cup green onion slices
8	corn tortillas
	Oil
¾	lb. *VELVEETA Mexican Pasteurized Process Cheese Spread with Jalapeño Pepper*, cubed
½	cup chopped tomato
¼	cup milk

▶ Mix together turkey, cream cheese and onions until well blended.

▶ Brush tortillas lightly with oil.

▶ Stack 4 tortillas on plate. Microwave on HIGH 30 seconds or until soft; repeat with remaining tortillas.

▶ Fill each tortilla with ¼ cup turkey mixture. Roll up; place, seam side down, in 12x8-inch baking dish.

▶ Microwave process cheese spread, tomatoes and milk on HIGH 2 to 4 minutes or until process cheese spread is melted, stirring after each minute.

▶ Pour sauce over tortillas; microwave on HIGH 12 to 14 minutes or until thoroughly heated, turning dish after 6 minutes. Garnish with cilantro, if desired.   4 servings

Variation: Substitute *LOUIS RICH Oven Roasted Boneless Turkey Breast* for cooked chicken or turkey.

Corned Beef & Cabbage Casserole

Prep time: 20 minutes
Conventional cooking time: 40 minutes
Microwave cooking time: 17 minutes

2	cups mashed potatoes
¼	cup chopped parsley
2	cups finely chopped cabbage
1½	cups finely chopped cooked corned beef
1	cup (4 ozs.) *VELVEETA Shredded Pasteurized Process Cheese Food*
½	cup shredded carrot
¼	cup chopped onion
1	teaspoon caraway seed (optional)

▶ Preheat oven to 350°.

▶ Mix together potatoes and parsley; spoon into 2-quart casserole.

▶ Mix together remaining ingredients; spoon over potatoes.

▶ Bake 35 to 40 minutes or until thoroughly heated. 6 servings

Microwave:

▶ Mix together potatoes and parsley; spoon into 2-quart casserole.

▶ Mix together remaining ingredients; spoon over potatoes.

▶ Microwave on HIGH 8 to 12 minutes or until thoroughly heated.

▶ Let stand 5 minutes before serving.

Ham and Cheese Calzones (below)

Prep time: 20 minutes
Cooking time: 12 minutes

1	small onion, chopped
2	tablespoons *PARKAY Margarine*
2	cups frozen Southern-style hash brown potatoes, thawed
1½	cups ham cubes
1	cup (4 ozs.) *VELVEETA Shredded Pasteurized Process Cheese Food*
1	tablespoon spicy brown mustard
1	(10 oz.) can refrigerated pizza crust

▶ Preheat oven to 400°.

▶ Saute onions in margarine .

▶ Add potatoes; continue cooking 3 to 5 minutes or until thoroughly heated. Remove from heat.

▶ Stir in all remaining ingredients except dough; mix well.

▶ Unroll dough; cut into four rectangles. Flatten each rectangle into 7-inch square.

▶ Place ¾ cup ham mixture on half of each square.

▶ Fold dough over filling to form triangle; press edges with fork to seal.

▶ Place on greased cookie sheet.

▶ Bake 10 to 12 minutes or until golden brown.   4 servings

Ham and Cheese Calzones

Not Just For Breakfast

Omelets, frittatas, stratas and quiche aren't *just* for breakfast. These extra-special egg dishes make great suppertime fare in a jiffy.

Vegetable Omelet

Helpful Hints

✓ Purchase clean, fresh eggs from a refrigerated display case. At home, refrigerate eggs immediately, discarding any with cracked shells.

✓ Add fruit or a salad and bread for a complete meal.

✓ Eggs in the shell can be safely stored in the refrigerator 4 to 5 weeks beyond the pack date stamped on the carton.

✓ Four ounces of natural or process cheese equal 1 cup when shredded. To measure, pack lightly in 1 cup measure.

Vegetable Omelet (opposite)

Prep time: 10 minutes
Cooking time: 10 minutes

½	cup chopped onion
½	cup mushroom slices
¼	cup chopped green pepper
¼	cup chopped red pepper
2	tablespoons *PARKAY Margarine*
½	cup chopped seeded tomato
	Few drops hot pepper sauce
4	eggs, beaten
2	tablespoons milk
2	*VELVEETA Slices Pasteurized Process Cheese Spread*, cut in half diagonally

▶ Saute onions, mushrooms and peppers in 1 tablespoon margarine in 10-inch skillet over medium-high heat until tender. Stir in tomatoes and hot pepper sauce; remove mixture from skillet.

▶ Melt remaining margarine in skillet. Mix together eggs and milk; pour into skillet.

▶ As egg mixture sets, lift slightly with spatula to allow uncooked portion to flow underneath.

▶ When egg mixture is set but top is still moist, place vegetables and process cheese spread on half of omelet.

▶ Slip spatula underneath, tip skillet to loosen and gently fold in half.   2 servings

Cheese and Sausage Strata

Prep time: 20 minutes plus chilling
Cooking time: 55 minutes plus standing

½	lb. bulk pork sausage
¾	cup mushroom slices
¼	cup green onion slices
½	lb. *VELVEETA Pasteurized Process Cheese Spread*, cubed
4	cups fresh sourdough bread cubes
1	cup milk
4	eggs, beaten

▶ Brown sausage; drain.

▶ Add vegetables, continue cooking 5 minutes. Drain. Cool 10 minutes.

▶ Mix together sausage mixture, process cheese spread and bread cubes. Spoon into greased 8-inch square baking dish.

▶ Beat milk and eggs; pour over sausage mixture.

▶ Cover; refrigerate several hours or overnight.

▶ Bake at 350°, uncovered, 50 to 55 minutes or until golden brown. Let stand 10 minutes before serving.   4 to 6 servings

Sensational Spinach Pie (below)

Prep time: 20 minutes
Cooking time: 40 minutes

1	lb. Italian sausage, casing removed, cooked, drained, crumbled
1	(15 oz.) container ricotta cheese
1	(10 oz.) pkg. *BIRDS EYE Chopped Spinach*, thawed, well drained
1	(8 oz.) container *PHILADELPHIA BRAND Soft Cream Cheese with Herb & Garlic*
1	cup (4 ozs.) *100% Natural KRAFT Shredded Low-Moisture Part-Skim Mozzarella Cheese*
3	eggs
½	teaspoon hot pepper sauce
1	(15 oz.) pkg. refrigerated pie crusts (2 crusts)

▶ Preheat oven to 400°.

▶ Mix together sausage, ricotta cheese, spinach, cream cheese, mozzarella cheese, two eggs and hot pepper sauce in large bowl until well blended.

▶ On lightly floured surface, roll out one pie crust to 12-inch circle. Place in 10-inch pie plate; fill with sausage mixture.

▶ Roll remaining pie crust to 12-inch circle; make decorative cut outs in pastry, if desired. Place pastry over filling. Seal and flute edges of pie. Decorate top with additional pie crust, cut into decorative shapes, if desired. Beat remaining egg; brush top of pastry.

▶ Bake 35 to 40 minutes or until pastry is lightly browned. Serve warm or at room temperature.   10 servings

Sensational Spinach Pie

Main Dish Salads

A main dish salad can fit *any* schedule. Some are best eaten right away; others benefit from being chilled to let their flavors blend. All offer a welcome change of pace from hot meat and potatoes fare.

Delicious Beef Salad

Helpful Hints

✓ Forgot to make ahead? Just set covered bowl in the freezer for a few minutes for a quick chill.

✓ Rinse hot cooked pasta with cold water; drain well before using.

✓ Mayonnaise and salad dressing can be used interchangeably in salad recipes.

✓ Vary the flavor by substituting one pourable dressing for another.

Delicious Beef Salad (opposite)
Prep time: 20 minutes plus chilling

1	(8 oz.) bottle *CATALINA French Dressing*
½	teaspoon chili powder
½	teaspoon dried oregano leaves
½	teaspoon ground cumin
8	Romaine or iceberg lettuce leaves, shredded
½	lb. roast beef, cut into strips
½	small red onion, thinly sliced
½	medium green or red pepper, cut into thin strips
1	(10 oz.) pkg. *BIRDS EYE Sweet Corn*, thawed, drained
4	ozs. *CASINO Natural Monterey Jack Cheese*, cut into ½-inch cubes
1	(2¼ oz.) can sliced pitted ripe olives, drained (approx. ½ cup)

▶ Mix together dressing and spices; chill.

▶ Arrange lettuce, roast beef, onions, peppers, corn, cheese and olives on large serving platter. Chill.

▶ Serve salad with dressing mixture.   4 servings

Chinese Chicken Salad
Prep time: 20 minutes plus chilling

½	cup *KRAFT Real Mayonnaise*
1	tablespoon soy sauce
½	teaspoon ground ginger
4	large pieces fried chicken, chilled, chopped (approx. 3 cups)
1	cup pea pods, sliced lengthwise, blanched
½	cup shredded carrot
¼	cup chopped green onions
1	tablespoon sesame seed, toasted
3	cups shredded lettuce

▶ Mix together mayonnaise, soy sauce and ginger in large bowl.

▶ Add chicken, pea pods, carrots, onions and sesame seeds; mix lightly. Chill.

▶ Serve on lettuce-covered platter.   4 servings

Variation: Substitute 3 cups chopped cooked chicken for fried chicken.

Marinated Ravioli
Vegetable Platter (below)
Prep time: 20 minutes plus chilling

1	(8 oz.) bottle *SEVEN SEAS VIVA ITALIAN! Reduced Calorie Dressing*
1	cup mushroom slices
1	cup red pepper strips
1	cup zucchini slices, cut in half
1	(2¼ oz.) can sliced pitted ripe olives, drained (approx. ½ cup)
2	(7 oz.) pkgs. dried cheese-filled ravioli, cooked, drained, chilled
½	cup (2 ozs.) *KRAFT 100% Grated Parmesan Cheese*
1½	qts. torn assorted greens

▶ Pour dressing over combined mushrooms, peppers, zucchini and olives. Cover; marinate in refrigerator several hours or overnight. Drain, reserving dressing.

▶ Toss together vegetable mixture, ravioli and ¼ cup cheese.

▶ Spoon vegetable mixture onto greens-covered serving platter; sprinkle with remaining cheese. Serve with reserved dressing.
4 to 6 servings

Variation: Substitute *SEVEN SEAS VIVA ITALIAN! Dressing* or *KRAFT House Italian Dressing* for reduced calorie dressing.

Marinated Ravioli Vegetable Platter

Main Dish Salads
(continued)

Shrimp and Rice Salad

Shrimp and Rice Salad (opposite)
Prep time: 15 minutes plus chilling

3	cups cooked *MINUTE Premium Long Grain Rice*
1	(10 oz.) pkg. *BIRDS EYE Green Peas,* thawed, drained
1	lb. cooked medium shrimp
1	cup *KRAFT LIGHT Cholesterol Free Reduced Calorie Mayonnaise*
½	cup chopped red pepper
2	tablespoons chopped onion
¼	teaspoon lemon pepper seasoning

▶ Mix together ingredients until well blended; chill.

6 to 8 servings

Texicali Salad
Prep/cooking time: 20 minutes

½	lb. ground beef
1	(8 oz.) can kidney beans, undrained
1	qt. shredded lettuce
1	cup (4 ozs.) *VELVEETA Mexican Shredded Pasteurized Process Cheese Food with Jalapeño Pepper*
1	cup chopped avocado
1	cup chopped tomato
¼	cup green onion slices
½	cup *CATALINA French Dressing*
3½	cups (4 ozs.) broken tortilla chips

▶ Brown meat, drain. Stir in beans; simmer 10 minutes.

▶ Mix together meat mixture, lettuce, process cheese food, avocados, tomatoes and onions. Add dressing and chips; mix lightly. Serve immediately.   6 servings

Southwest Chicken Salad (below)
Prep time: 20 minutes
Cooking time: 20 minutes

½	cup *SEVEN SEAS VIVA ITALIAN! Dressing*
½	cup *SEVEN SEAS VIVA RANCH! Dressing*
⅛	to ¼ teaspoon ground red pepper
4	(approx. 1¼ lbs.) boneless skinless chicken breasts
1	avocado, peeled, cut into chunks
1	red pepper, cut into strips
1½	qts. shredded lettuce
2	tablespoons chopped cilantro (optional)

▶ Stir together dressings and ground red pepper; reserve ½ cup.

▶ Pour remaining dressing mixture over chicken. Cover; marinate in refrigerator 2 to 3 hours.

▶ Preheat electric broiler (not necessary to preheat gas broiler).

▶ Remove chicken from marinade; discard marinade.

▶ Place chicken on greased rack of broiler pan 4 to 5 inches from heat. Broil 8 to 10 minutes on each side or until tender. Cut into strips.

▶ Arrange chicken, avocados and red peppers over lettuce on large serving platter. Sprinkle with cilantro. Serve with reserved ½ cup dressing mixture.   4 to 6 servings

Southwest Chicken Salad

Savory Soups and Breads

A steaming bowl of soup accompanied by special bread will warm up a chilly night. We've kept the rich aromas and hearty flavors but streamlined the preparation.

Creamy Potato Soup, Zesty French Bread

Helpful Hints

✓ Dress up a bowl of soup with one of these good food ideas: shredded cheese, a dollop of sour cream, plain or seasoned croutons, chow mein noodles, sliced green onion or chopped parsley.

✓ Keep bread warm at the table by serving in a napkin-lined basket.

✓ To warm leftover bread, wrap in foil and heat in the oven at 400° or wrap in a white paper towel and microwave on HIGH just until warm to the touch.

Creamy Potato Soup (opposite)

Prep time: 5 minutes
Cooking time: 25 minutes

6	*OSCAR MAYER Bacon Slices*, chopped
1	small onion, chopped
2½	cups cold water
1	(5.75 oz.) pkg. *KRAFT Au Gratin Potatoes & Cheese*
2	cups milk
1	tablespoon chopped parsley
	Dash of pepper

▶ Cook bacon and onions in 3-quart saucepan. Drain; remove from pan.

▶ In same pan, bring water to boil. Add Potatoes.

▶ Simmer, uncovered, over medium heat 18 minutes.

▶ Stir in Sauce Mix, milk, parsley, pepper, bacon and onions. Simmer over medium heat 4 to 5 minutes or until desired consistency. Four (1 cup) servings

Salsa Corn Chowder (right)

Prep time: 5 minutes
Cooking time: 35 minutes

1½	cups chopped onion
2	tablespoons *PARKAY Margarine*
1	tablespoon flour
1	tablespoon chili powder
1	teaspoon ground cumin
1	(16 oz.) pkg. *BIRDS EYE Sweet Corn*, thawed
2	cups salsa
1	(13¾ oz.) can chicken broth
1	(4 oz.) jar chopped pimento, drained
1	(8 oz.) container *PHILADELPHIA BRAND Soft Cream Cheese*
1	cup milk
	Cilantro (optional)

▶ Saute onions in margarine in large saucepan. Stir in flour and spices.

▶ Add corn, salsa, broth and pimentos. Bring to boil; remove from heat.

▶ Gradually add ¼ cup hot mixture to cream cheese in small bowl, stirring until well blended.

▶ Return cream cheese mixture to saucepan; stir in milk until well blended.

▶ Cook until thoroughly heated; do not boil. Top each serving with cilantro, if desired. Serve immediately. 6 to 8 servings

Zesty French Bread (opposite)

Prep/cooking time: 9 minutes

1	(16-inch) French bread loaf, cut in half horizontally
¼	cup *SEVEN SEAS VIVA ITALIAN! Dressing*
2	cups (8 ozs.) shredded *CASINO Natural Low-Moisture Part-Skim Mozzarella Cheese*
2	teaspoons finely chopped fresh basil

▶ Brush cut side of bread with dressing; top with cheese and basil.

▶ Broil 3 to 4 minutes or until cheese begins to melt. Cut into 2-inch slices. 16 servings

Variation: Substitute ½ teaspoon dried basil leaves for fresh basil.

Parmesan Twists (below)

Prep time: 10 minutes
Cooking time: 10 minutes

1	(8 oz.) can refrigerated quick crescent dinner rolls
½	cup (2 ozs.) *KRAFT 100% Grated Parmesan Cheese*

▶ Preheat oven to 375°.

▶ Unroll dough and separate into four rectangles; firmly press perforations to seal.

▶ Sprinkle both sides of each rectangle with cheese; cut into six lengthwise strips. Twist strips; place on greased cookie sheet.

▶ Bake 7 to 10 minutes or until lightly browned. 2 dozen

Variation: For appetizer twists, cut each strip in half.
Note: For crisper twists, bake a day in advance and store in loosely covered container.

Salsa Corn Chowder, Parmesan Twists

Savory Soups
and Breads
(continued)

Creamy Vegetable Ham Soup, Garlic Bread

Creamy Vegetable Ham Soup (opposite)

Prep time: 10 minutes
Conventional cooking time: 20 minutes
Microwave cooking time: 18 minutes

¾   cup chopped onion
1   tablespoon *PARKAY Margarine*
1   (13¾ oz.) can chicken broth
1   cup milk
¾   lb. *VELVEETA Pasteurized Process Cheese Spread,* cubed
1   (16 oz.) pkg. *BIRDS EYE Mixed Vegetables,* thawed, drained
2   cups ham cubes
     Dash of pepper

▶ Saute onions in margarine in 2-quart saucepan.

▶ Add broth, milk and process cheese spread. Stir over low heat until process cheese spread is melted.

▶ Stir in vegetables, ham and pepper; cover. Cook until thoroughly heated, stirring occasionally.   Six (1 cup) servings

Microwave:

▶ Microwave onions in margarine in 2-quart bowl on HIGH 2 minutes.

▶ Add broth, milk and process cheese spread. Cover with plastic wrap; vent. Microwave on HIGH 5 to 7 minutes or until process cheese spread is melted, stirring after 3 minutes.

▶ Add vegetables, ham and pepper. Cover with plastic wrap; vent. Microwave on HIGH 7 to 9 minutes or until thoroughly heated, stirring every 3 minutes.

Garlic Bread (opposite)

Prep time: 10 minutes
Cooking time: 15 minutes

1   (16-inch) French bread loaf, cut into 1-inch slices
½   cup *PARKAY Spread*
1   teaspoon garlic salt

▶ Preheat oven to 400°.

▶ Spread one side of each bread slice with combined spread and garlic salt. Place bread, spread-side up, on ungreased cookie sheet.

▶ Bake 12 to 15 minutes or until lightly browned.   16 servings

Variation: Add 1 teaspoon dried basil or oregano leaves to spread mixture.

Onion Soup Gratinee (below)

Prep time: 10 minutes
Cooking time: 30 minutes

3   cups fresh onion rings
2   tablespoons *PARKAY Margarine*
2   (10½ oz.) cans condensed beef broth
2½   cups cold water
     Dash of pepper
6   French bread slices, toasted
1   (8 oz.) pkg. *100% Natural KRAFT Swiss Cheese Slices*
     KRAFT 100% Grated Parmesan Cheese

▶ Saute onions in margarine in large saucepan 10 minutes or until tender. Add broth, water and pepper. Cover; simmer 15 minutes.

▶ Pour soup into six 8-ounce ovenproof serving bowls; top with bread slices. Cover with Swiss and parmesan cheeses. Place bowls on jelly roll pan.

▶ Broil 3 minutes or until Swiss cheese is melted and golden brown. Serve immediately.   Six (1 cup) servings

Onion Soup Gratinee

Sensational Sandwiches

The Earl of Sandwich would be proud of these classics. The kids will eat them right up.

Ham And Cheese Croissants, Waldorf Salad

Helpful Hints

✓ For a more substantial meal, add deli coleslaw, potato salad or a cup of soup.

✓ Use a serrated knife and firm gentle pressure to neatly slice tomatoes.

✓ Line pita pockets with leaf lettuce, spinach or romaine before adding the filling.

✓ Store bread and rolls in resealable freezer bags. To thaw, remove from bag and wrap in paper towel. Microwave on HIGH just until no longer cold.

Ham And Cheese Croissants (opposite)

Prep time: 15 minutes

⅓ cup green onion slices
¼ cup **KRAFT Real Mayonnaise**
¼ cup **SAUCEWORKS Horseradish Sauce**
6 croissants, split
   Lettuce
   Tomato slices
2 (6 oz.) pkgs. **OSCAR MAYER Smoked Ham Slices**
6 **VELVEETA Slices Pasteurized Process Cheese Spread, cut in half diagonally**

▶ Mix together onion, mayonnaise and horseradish sauce; chill.

▶ For each sandwich, spread approximately 1 tablespoon of mayonnaise mixture on croissant; fill with lettuce, tomato, ham and process cheese spread.   6 sandwiches

Variation: Microwave two sandwiches on paper towel on HIGH 1 minute or until process cheese spread is melted.

Cheddar Sloppy Joes

Prep time: 5 minutes
Cooking time: 15 minutes

1 lb. ground beef
½ cup chopped green pepper
¼ cup chopped onion
1 (10.5 oz.) container **SPREADERY Cheese Snack Medium Cheddar Cold Pack Cheese Product**
1 (14½ oz.) can tomatoes, drained, cut up
6 hamburger buns or Kaiser rolls, split

▶ Brown meat; drain. Add peppers and onions; cook until tender.

▶ Stir in cheese snack and tomatoes; cook over low heat until thoroughly heated.

▶ Fill buns with meat mixture.   6 sandwiches

Club Sandwich

Prep time: 15 minutes

12 bread slices, toasted
   KRAFT Real Mayonnaise
2 100% **Natural KRAFT Sharp Cheddar Cheese Slices, cut in half**
1 (16 oz.) pkg. **OSCAR MAYER Thin Sliced Chicken Breast**
   Lettuce

2 100% **Natural KRAFT Swiss Cheese Slices, cut in half**
8 tomato slices
12 **OSCAR MAYER Bacon Slices, crisply cooked**

▶ For each sandwich, spread three toast slices with mayonnaise.

▶ Cover one toast slice with cheddar cheese, chicken, lettuce and second toast slice. Top with Swiss cheese, tomato, bacon and third toast slice.

▶ Cut in quarters; secure with wooden picks.   4 sandwiches

Parmesan Crab Cakes (below)

Prep time: 15 minutes
Cooking time: 6 minutes

1 (8 oz.) pkg. **LOUIS KEMP Crab Delight Flakes, rinsed, chopped**
1 cup (4 ozs.) **KRAFT 100% Grated Parmesan Cheese**
2 eggs, beaten
½ cup finely chopped red or green pepper
½ cup finely chopped green onion
1 teaspoon Dijon mustard
½ cup dry bread crumbs
¼ cup oil
   SAUCEWORKS Natural Lemon & Herb Flavor Tartar Sauce
8 sourdough bread slices, toasted

▶ Mix together first six ingredients until well blended. Shape mixture into eight 3-inch patties. Coat with bread crumbs.

▶ Heat oil in large skillet over medium-high heat. Cook patties 3 minutes on each side or until golden brown.

▶ For each sandwich, spread two bread slices with tartar sauce. Top one bread slice with two patties and second bread slice. 4 sandwiches

Parmesan Crab Cakes, Honey Mustard Coleslaw

Sensational
Sandwiches
(continued)

Vegetable Turkey Pockets

Vegetable Turkey Pockets (opposite)

Prep time: 20 minutes plus chilling

¼ cup *SEVEN SEAS VIVA RANCH! Reduced Calorie Dressing*
¼ cup *KRAFT LIGHT Cholesterol Free Reduced Calorie Mayonnaise*
1½ cups *LOUIS RICH Oven Roasted Boneless Turkey Breast Strips*
½ cup shredded carrot
½ cup chopped cucumber
1 small tomato, chopped
2 whole wheat pita bread rounds, cut in half
  Lettuce

▶ Mix together dressing, mayonnaise, turkey, carrots, cucumber and tomatoes. Chill. Fill bread with lettuce and turkey mixture. 4 sandwiches

Tuna Sandwich Melts

Prep time: 15 minutes
Cooking time: 25 minutes

½ cup *MIRACLE WHIP Salad Dressing*
1 (6½ oz.) can tuna in water, drained
½ cup (¼ lb.) cubed *VELVEETA Pasteurized Process Cheese Spread*
½ cup chopped celery
¼ cup chopped onion
6 hamburger buns, split

▶ Preheat oven to 375°.
▶ Mix together all ingredients except buns.
▶ Fill buns with ⅓ cup tuna mixture; wrap in foil.
▶ Bake 20 to 25 minutes or until thoroughly heated.
6 sandwiches

Microwave:
▶ Prepare sandwiches as directed except for wrapping in foil.
▶ Place two sandwiches on paper towel.
▶ Microwave on HIGH 1 minute or until thoroughly heated.

Favorite Reubens (below)

Prep time: 5 minutes
Cooking time: 15 minutes

8 rye bread slices
2 (6 oz.) pkgs. *OSCAR MAYER Corned Beef Slices*
1 (8 oz.) can sauerkraut, drained
8 *VELVEETA Slices Pasteurized Process Cheese Spread*
¼ cup *KRAFT Thousand Island Dressing*
  PARKAY Soft Margarine

▶ For each sandwich, cover one bread slice with 1½ ozs. meat, approximately ¼ cup sauerkraut, 1½ ozs. meat, 2 slices process cheese spread, 1 tablespoon dressing and second bread slice.

▶ Spread sandwich with margarine. Grill until lightly browned on both sides. 4 sandwiches

Favorite Reubens

◀ **Problem:**

You've decided on the
main dish, now what about
an accompaniment?

▲ **Solution:**

Stop singing those side dish blues, add a pasta salad,
rice with "mix-ins" or Cheesy Mashed Potatoes. Choose
any of our quick side dishes and watch everyone dig in.

Super

Side

Dishes

Jazz-up a simple entree like broiled chicken or fish with a special side dish or salad. We've selected our favorites, now you select yours.

Jazzed Up Veggies

Why settle for steamed broccoli or plain mashed potatoes when you can jazz-up your favorites – fast – with a few simple ingredients. These quick fixer-uppers use pasteurized process cheese spread, pourable dressings, cream cheese and crunchies like potato chips and crushed corn flakes.

Cheese & Broccoli with Crunchy Toppings

Helpful Hints

✓ Eliminate last minute chopping by cleaning and slicing the fresh vegetables you plan to use within 2 or 3 days when you bring them home from the market. Pat dry with paper towels and store in resealable plastic bags.

✓ Top a baked potato with one of these good food ideas: sour cream and bacon bits, shredded cheddar and sliced green onion, cooked frozen broccoli and pasteurized process cheese spread, Italian dressing and sliced black olives, chopped tomato and parmesan cheese. Or, borrow a topping idea from *Burgers and Toppers* (page 15).

Cheese & Broccoli with Crunchy Toppings (opposite)
Prep/cooking time: 15 minutes

1   (8 oz.) jar *CHEEZ WHIZ Pasteurized Process Cheese Spread*
2   (10 oz.) pkgs. *BIRDS EYE Broccoli Spears*, cooked, drained
½   cup topping (*OSCAR MAYER Bacon Slices*, crisply cooked, crumbled, chopped nuts, crushed crackers, seasoned croutons or crushed potato or corn chips)

▶ Heat process cheese spread according to label directions.
▶ Pour over broccoli spears. Sprinkle with topping.   6 to 8 servings

Spinach in Cream Sauce
Prep time: 10 minutes
Cooking time: 5 minutes

1   (8 oz.) pkg. *PHILADELPHIA BRAND Cream Cheese*, cubed
2   tablespoons *PARKAY Margarine*
2   tablespoons milk
½   teaspoon salt
¼   teaspoon hot pepper sauce
2   (10 oz.) pkgs. *BIRDS EYE Chopped Spinach*, cooked, well drained
1   hard-cooked egg, finely chopped (optional)

▶ Stir together cream cheese, margarine, milk, salt and hot pepper sauce over low heat until smooth. Add spinach; heat thoroughly. Top with egg.   6 to 8 servings

Italian Grilled Vegetables (right)
Prep time: 10 minutes
Cooking time: 12 minutes

½   cup *MIRACLE WHIP Salad Dressing*
½   cup *SEVEN SEAS VIVA ITALIAN! Dressing*
2   zucchini, cut in half lengthwise
2   summer squash, cut in half lengthwise
2   red, green or yellow peppers, cut into quarters

▶ Preheat electric broiler (not necessary to preheat gas broiler).
▶ Mix together dressings until well blended.
▶ Lightly score cut sides of vegetables; brush one side with salad dressing mixture.

▶ Place vegetables, salad dressing side up, on rack of broiler pan 4 inches from heat.   Broil 6 minutes.   Turn; brush with salad dressing mixture. Continue broiling 6 minutes or until vegetables are tender.   4 to 6 servings

Variations: Substitute *MIRACLE WHIP LIGHT Cholesterol Free Reduced Calorie Salad Dressing* for regular salad dressing. Substitute *SEVEN SEAS VIVA! Reduced Calorie Dressing* for Italian dressing.

Cheesy Mashed Potatoes (pictured on page 17)
Prep/cooking time: 10 minutes

2   cups instant potato flakes
1   (8 oz.) jar *CHEEZ WHIZ Pasteurized Process Cheese Spread*
⅓   cup sour cream
⅓   cup chopped green onions

▶ Prepare potatoes according to package directions, except omit milk.
▶ Heat process cheese spread according to label directions.
▶ Stir together ingredients until well blended.   4 to 6 servings

Variation: Omit sour cream.

Classic Vegetable Toss
Prep/cooking time: 10 minutes

1   (16 oz.) pkg. *BIRDS EYE Farm Fresh Vegetables*
⅓   cup *SEVEN SEAS VIVA RANCH! Dressing*

▶ Cook vegetables according to package directions; drain. Toss with dressing.   6 to 8 servings

Italian Grilled Vegetables

Plan Ahead Salads

A salad adds color, crunch and a "nutrition boost" to any menu. This collection features make-aheads like coleslaw and potato salad and an antipasto salad that can double as a light main dish.

Antipasto Salad

Helpful Hints

✓ Purchase shredded cabbage for coleslaw at the produce section.

✓ Keep a "greens mix"– torn spinach, romaine and iceberg lettuce – on hand in the refrigerator. Wash and spin dry greens; store in a resealable plastic bag. Toss with a pourable dressing for an instant salad.

✓ A salad spinner quick-dries salad greens, fresh herbs and leafy vegetables.

✓ Planned over meats like sliced roast beef, ham or turkey breast can be used in the antipasto salad.

✓ Pair two of the salads with cold cuts for a deli supper.

Antipasto Salad (opposite)

Prep time: 15 minutes plus chilling

3	cups (8 ozs.) medium shell macaroni, cooked, drained
½	cup *SEVEN SEAS VIVA ITALIAN! Dressing*
4	ozs. *CASINO Natural Low-Moisture Part-Skim Mozzarella Cheese*, cubed
4	*OSCAR MAYER Cotto Salami Slices*, cut into strips
½	cup pitted ripe olives
½	cup red pepper strips
½	cup zucchini strips

▶ Toss together pasta and dressing.

▶ Arrange remaining ingredients over pasta; chill.   8 servings

Easy Cheesy Macaroni Salad

Prep time: 10 minutes plus chilling

1	(8 oz.) jar *CHEEZ WHIZ Pasteurized Process Cheese Spread*
¼	cup *KRAFT Real Mayonnaise*
¼	teaspoon ground celery seed
2	cups (7 ozs.) elbow macaroni, cooked, drained
1	cup seeded chopped tomato
½	cup chopped cucumber
¼	cup chopped onion

▶ Heat process cheese spread according to label directions. Mix with mayonnaise and celery seed in large bowl.

▶ Stir in remaining ingredients; chill.

▶ Add additional mayonnaise and sprinkle with additional celery seed before serving, if desired.   4 to 6 servings

Carrot Raisin Mallow Salad

Prep time: 10 minutes plus chilling

3	cups shredded carrots
1½	cups *KRAFT Miniature Marshmallows*
⅔	cup raisins
½	cup *MIRACLE WHIP Salad Dressing*
½	cup celery slices
¼	cup coarsely chopped walnuts

▶ Mix together ingredients lightly; chill.   8 to 10 servings

Pineapple Lime Mold (below)

Prep time: 15 minutes plus chilling

1½	cups cold water
1	(3 oz.) pkg. *JELL-O Lime Flavored Gelatin Dessert*
1	tablespoon lemon juice
1	(8 oz.) pkg. *PHILADELPHIA BRAND Cream Cheese*, softened
2	(8 oz.) cans crushed pineapple, drained
1½	cups *KRAFT Miniature Marshmallows*
½	cup chopped nuts (optional)
	Shredded lettuce

▶ Bring 1 cup water to boil; stir in gelatin until dissolved. Add remaining ½ cup water and juice.

▶ Gradually add gelatin to cream cheese, mixing until blended.

▶ Chill until thickened but not set; fold in pineapple, marshmallows and nuts. Pour into 1-quart mold; chill until firm. Unmold onto serving plate; surround with lettuce. Serve with assorted fresh fruit and nuts, if desired.   6 servings

Variation: Omit lemon juice. Substitute one (8 oz.) container plain yogurt for cream cheese.

Pineapple Lime Mold

Plan Ahead Salads
(continued)

Layered Salad

Layered Salad (opposite)
Prep time: 10 minutes plus chilling

1	**qt. shredded lettuce**
1	**pt. cherry tomatoes, quartered**
1	**(10 oz.) pkg. *BIRDS EYE Mixed Vegetables*, thawed, drained**
1	**cup *KRAFT Real Mayonnaise***
¼	**cup (1 oz.) *KRAFT 100% Grated Parmesan Cheese***
4	***OSCAR MAYER Bacon Slices*, crisply cooked, crumbled (optional)**

▶ Layer lettuce, tomatoes and vegetables in 2½-quart serving bowl.

▶ Mix together mayonnaise and cheese; spread over salad to seal. Cover; chill. Sprinkle with bacon just before serving.   8 servings

Waldorf Salad (pictured on page 38)
Prep time: 10 minutes plus chilling

3	**cups chopped red and green apples**
½	**cup *KRAFT Real Mayonnaise* or *MIRACLE WHIP Salad Dressing***
½	**cup coarsely chopped walnuts**
½	**cup raisins**
½	**cup thawed *COOL WHIP Whipped Topping***

▶ Mix together apples, mayonnaise, walnuts and raisins. Fold in whipped topping; chill.   4 to 6 servings

Honey Mustard Coleslaw (pictured on page 39)
Prep time: 15 minutes plus chilling

¾	**cup *KRAFT Real Mayonnaise***
1	**tablespoon honey**
2	**teaspoons Dijon mustard**
5	**cups shredded green cabbage**
1	**cup shredded carrots**

▶ Mix together mayonnaise, honey and mustard in large bowl.

▶ Stir in remaining ingredients; chill.   6 servings

Microwave Potato Salad (below)
Prep time: 20 minutes plus chilling
Microwave cooking time: 18 minutes

7	**cups (2½ lbs.) cubed red potatoes**
⅓	**cup cold water**
¾	**cup *KRAFT Real Mayonnaise* or *MIRACLE WHIP Salad Dressing***
¾	**cup (3 ozs.) *100% Natural KRAFT Shredded Cheddar Cheese***
¾	**cup (3 ozs.) *100% Natural KRAFT Shredded Swiss Cheese***
½	**cup green onion slices**
¼	**cup milk**
2	**hard-cooked eggs, chopped**
½	**teaspoon salt**
½	**teaspoon pepper**

▶ Place potatoes and water in 3-quart casserole; cover.

▶ Microwave on HIGH 16 to 18 minutes or until tender, stirring after 9 minutes. Drain.

▶ Stir in remaining ingredients; chill.   6 to 8 servings

Microwave Potato Salad

Mix-Ins For Pasta and Rice

Dress-up plain pasta and rice with an ingredient or two from the pantry and fridge. Start with frozen vegetables, cheese and pourable dressings, then use your imagination to create new flavor combinations your family will love.

Risotto with Sausage

Helpful Hints

✓ Create instant eye appeal by combining quick cooking white and brown rice or two different pasta shapes.

✓ Vary the cheese and frozen vegetable in *Garden Vegetable Pasta Salad.*

✓ All out of cream of mushroom soup? Use cream of celery, cream of chicken or cream of onion in *Broccoli 'N Rice Casserole.*

✓ Use any vegetables you have on hand in *Italian Pasta Salad;* toss with your favorite pourable dressing.

Risotto with Sausage (opposite)

Prep/cooking time: 15 minutes plus standing
Microwave cooking time: 12 minutes plus standing

½   lb. Italian sausage, casing removed
½   cup chopped onion
1 ⅔ cups cold water
½   teaspoon dried oregano leaves, crushed
1 ⅔ cups *MINUTE Premium Long Grain Rice*
2   tablespoons chopped parsley
1   cup (4 ozs.) *VELVEETA Shredded Pasteurized Process Cheese Food*

▶ Brown sausage; drain.

▶ Add onions; cook until tender.

▶ Stir in water and oregano; bring to full boil.

▶ Stir in rice and parsley. Cover; remove from heat. Let stand 5 minutes; fluff with fork.

▶ Stir in process cheese food until melted. 6 servings

Microwave:

▶ Crumble sausage into 1½-quart casserole; stir in onions.

▶ Microwave on HIGH 3 to 5 minutes or until meat loses pink color when stirred; drain.

▶ Stir in water, oregano, rice and parsley.

▶ Cover; microwave on HIGH 5 to 7 minutes or until liquid is absorbed. Fluff with fork.

▶ Stir in process cheese food.

▶ Cover; let stand 5 minutes or until process cheese food is melted.

Creamy Rice and Tomatoes (right)

Prep/cooking time: 10 minutes

3   cups *MINUTE Rice*
1   (10.5 oz.) container *SPREADERY Cheese Snack Neufchatel Cheese with Classic Ranch Flavor*
1   (14½ oz.) can tomatoes, drained, cut up

▶ Cook rice according to package directions.

▶ Stir in cheese snack and tomatoes. 8 servings

Broccoli 'N Rice Casserole

Prep time: 5 minutes
Microwave cooking time: 12 minutes
Conventional cooking time: 40 minutes

1   (10 ¾ oz.) can condensed cream of mushroom soup
1   (10 oz.) pkg. *BIRDS EYE Chopped Broccoli,* thawed, drained
1   cup *MINUTE Rice*
1   (8 oz.) jar *CHEEZ WHIZ Pasteurized Process Cheese Spread*
1   cup French fried onions
¼   cup water

Microwave:

▶ Mix together soup, broccoli, rice, process cheese spread, ½ cup onions and water. Spoon into 1-quart casserole.

▶ Microwave on HIGH 4 minutes.

▶ Stir; top with remaining onions. Microwave on HIGH 6 to 8 minutes or until thoroughly heated. 6 servings

Conventional:

▶ Preheat oven to 350°.

▶ Mix together soup, broccoli, rice, process cheese spread, ½ cup onions and water. Spoon into 1-quart casserole.

▶ Bake 35 minutes.

▶ Top with remaining onions; continue baking 5 minutes.

Creamy Rice and Tomatoes

Mix-Ins For
Pasta and Rice
(continued)

Garden Vegetable Pasta Salad

Garden Vegetable Pasta Salad (opposite)

Prep/cooking time: 15 minutes

2	cups (5½ ozs.) rotini
1	(10.5 oz.) container *SPREADERY Cheese Snack Neufchatel Cheese with Garden Vegetables*
½	cup milk
1	(10 oz.) pkg. *BIRDS EYE Peas and Carrots*, thawed, drained
1	cup broccoli flowerets

▶ Cook pasta according to package directions. Rinse with COLD water; drain well.

▶ Mix together cheese snack and milk in large bowl.

▶ Add pasta and remaining ingredients; toss lightly. Serve immediately or chill.   6 servings

Italian Pasta Salad

Prep/cooking time: 15 minutes

3	cups (8 ozs.) radiatore or rotini pasta
1	cup *SEVEN SEAS VIVA RANCH! Dressing*
2	cups broccoli flowerets
½	cup chopped pitted ripe olives
½	cup chopped red pepper
⅓	cup chopped red onion

▶ Cook pasta according to package directions. Rinse with COLD water; drain well.

▶ Add remaining ingredients; toss lightly.

▶ Serve immediately or chill.   6 to 8 servings

Rice 'N Vegetables Parmesan

Prep time: 5 minutes
Cooking time: 15 minutes

⅓	cup chopped onion
2	tablespoons *PARKAY Margarine*
1	cup water
¼	teaspoon dried basil leaves, crushed
1	cup *MINUTE RICE*
1	(10 oz.) pkg. *BIRDS EYE Mixed Vegetables*, cooked, drained
⅓	cup (1½ ozs.) *KRAFT 100% Grated Parmesan Cheese*

▶ Saute onions in margarine. Add water and basil; bring to full boil.

▶ Stir in rice. Cover; remove from heat. Let stand 5 minutes; fluff with fork.

▶ Stir in vegetables and cheese.   6 servings

Noodles Romanoff

Prep/cooking time: 10 minutes

4	cups (8 ozs.) noodles
1	cup sour cream
½	cup (2 ozs.) *KRAFT 100% Grated Parmesan Cheese*

▶ Prepare noodles as directed on package; drain. Return to pan.

▶ Add remaining ingredients; toss lightly. Serve immediately. 6 to 8 servings

Fettucini Toss (below)

Prep/cooking time: 15 minutes plus standing

1	(6 oz.) pkg. *KRAFT Fettucini Alfredo Pasta & Cheese*
1	(10 oz.) pkg. *BIRDS EYE Green Peas*, thawed, drained
1	(4½ oz.) jar mushroom slices, drained

▶ Prepare Pasta & Cheese according to package directions, stirring in remaining ingredients during last minute of cooking.

▶ Remove from heat. Cover; let stand 2 minutes. 4 to 6 servings

Fettucini Toss

◄ Problem:

Cookie jar empty?
No time to bake?
What's a busy parent to do?

▲ Solution:

Fill it in a flash with sweet treats that can be made in a hurry...on the weekend...with the kids' help.

Sweets

And

Treats

End a meal on a sweet note, or satisfy a snack attack. *Caramelcorn* to *Outrageous Brownies*, all of these treats are quick, easy and oh so delicious.

For Chocolate Lovers

These chocolaty good treats use on-hand ingredients like caramels, marshmallows and chocolate. All can be made ahead, but the Rocky Road Fudge Sauce is last-minute quick.

Rocky Road Fudge Sauce

Helpful Hints

✓ For perfect results every time, use the microwave oven to melt chocolate. Place one 1 ounce square in small microwave-safe bowl. Microwave on HIGH 1 to 2 minutes. Chocolate will look shiny. Stir until melted and smooth.

✓ To easily remove marshmallow creme from jar, remove lid and seal. Microwave on HIGH 30 seconds.

✓ Freeze the *Outrageous Brownies* and *Chocolate Caramel Nut Bars* in airtight containers. Use waxed paper between layers for easy removal.

✓ Scoop ice cream into dessert dishes while the main dish heats. Cover with plastic wrap and place in freezer. At dessert time, uncover and top with *Rocky Road Fudge Sauce* or an ice cream topping from the pantry shelf.

Rocky Road Fudge Sauce (opposite)

Prep/cooking time: 6 minutes
Microwave cooking time: 4 minutes

1	(12 oz.) pkg. *BAKER'S Real Semi-Sweet Chocolate Chips*
1	(7 oz.) jar *KRAFT Marshmallow Creme*
1/3	cup milk
1/2	cup *KRAFT Miniature Marshmallows*
1/2	cup chopped pecans, toasted

▶ Stir together chocolate chips, marshmallow creme and milk in large saucepan over low heat until smooth.

▶ Stir in marshmallows and nuts; serve over ice cream, pound cake or angel food cake.   2 cups

Microwave:

▶ Microwave chocolate chips, marshmallow creme and milk on MEDIUM (50%) 3 to 4 minutes or until smooth, stirring every 1½ minutes.

▶ Stir in marshmallows and nuts.

Outrageous Brownies (right)

Prep time: 10 minutes
Cooking time: 35 minutes

1/2	cup *MIRACLE WHIP Salad Dressing*
2	eggs, beaten
1/4	cup water
1	(21.5 oz.) pkg. fudge brownie mix
5	(4 oz.) *BAKER'S GERMAN'S Sweet Chocolate* bars

▶ Preheat oven to 350°.

▶ Mix together salad dressing, eggs and water until well blended. Stir in brownie mix, mixing just until moistened.

▶ Coarsely chop four chocolate bars; stir into brownie mixture. Pour into greased 13 x 9-inch baking pan.

▶ Bake 30 to 35 minutes or until edges begin to pull away from sides of pan. Immediately top with one chopped chocolate bar. Let stand 5 minutes or until melted; spread evenly over brownies. Garnish with walnut halves, if desired. Cool. Cut into bars.   2 dozen

Chocolate Caramel Nut Bars

Prep time: 25 minutes
Cooking time: 18 minutes

1	(14 oz.) bag *KRAFT Caramels*
1	(5 fl. oz.) can evaporated milk
1	two-layer German chocolate cake mix with pudding
1/2	cup *PARKAY Margarine,* melted
1	cup *BAKER'S Real Semi-Sweet Chocolate Chips*
1½	cups chopped walnuts

▶ Preheat oven to 350°.

▶ Melt caramels with ⅓ cup milk in medium saucepan over low heat, stirring until smooth. Set aside.

▶ Mix together remaining milk, cake mix and margarine in large bowl. Press half of cake mixture onto bottom of ungreased 13 x 9-inch baking pan. Bake 8 minutes.

▶ Sprinkle chocolate chips and 1 cup walnuts over crust; top with caramel mixture, spreading to edges of pan. Top with teaspoonfuls of remaining cake mixture; press gently into caramel mixture. Sprinkle with remaining walnuts.

▶ Bake 16 to 18 minutes. Cool. Cut into bars.
Approximately 2 dozen

Microwave Tip: Microwave caramels with milk in 2-quart bowl on HIGH 3 to 4 minutes or until sauce is smooth, stirring every 2 minutes.

Variation: Substitute chocolate cake mix for German chocolate cake mix.

Outrageous Brownies

For Chocolate Lovers
(continued)

Chocolate Peanut Squares

Chocolate Peanut Squares (opposite)

Prep time: 30 minutes plus chilling

1	cup *PARKAY Margarine*
6	(1 oz.) squares *BAKER'S Semi-Sweet Chocolate*
1¾	cups graham cracker crumbs
1	cup *BAKER'S ANGEL FLAKE Coconut*
½	cup chopped unsalted peanuts
2	(8 oz.) pkgs. *PHILADELPHIA BRAND Cream Cheese*, softened
1	cup sugar
1	teaspoon vanilla

▶ Microwave ¾ cup margarine with 2 chocolate squares on HIGH 1 to 2 minutes or until melted when stirred, stirring every 30 seconds.

▶ Stir in crumbs, coconut and peanuts. Press onto bottom of 13 x 9-inch baking pan; chill 30 minutes.

▶ Mix together cream cheese, sugar and vanilla until well blended. Spread over crust; chill 30 minutes.

▶ Microwave remaining margarine and chocolate squares on HIGH 1 to 2 minutes or until melted when stirred, stirring every 30 seconds. Spread over cream cheese layer; chill. Cut into bars.   4 dozen

Chocolate Mousse

Prep time: 10 minutes plus chilling

1¾	cups cold milk
1	teaspoon *MAXWELL HOUSE Instant Coffee*
1	(8 oz.) pkg. *PHILADELPHIA BRAND Cream Cheese*, softened
1	(4 oz.) pkg. *JELL-O Chocolate Flavor Instant Pudding and Pie Filling*

▶ Microwave ¼ cup milk and coffee granules on HIGH 30 to 45 seconds or until coffee granules are dissolved when stirred.

▶ Gradually add coffee mixture and remaining milk to cream cheese, mixing at medium speed with electric mixer until well blended.

▶ Add pudding mix; mix at low speed with electric mixer 1 to 2 minutes or until well blended.

▶ Spoon into six parfait glasses or dessert dishes. Chill. Top with *COOL WHIP Whipped Topping*, thawed, if desired.   6 servings

Marshmallow Truffles (below)

Prep time: 30 minutes plus freezing
Microwave cooking time: 2½ minutes

1	(10 oz.) pkg. *KRAFT Jet-Puffed Marshmallows*
1	(12 oz.) pkg. *BAKER'S Real Semi-Sweet Chocolate Chips*
	BAKER'S ANGEL FLAKE Coconut, toasted
	Decorative candies

▶ Arrange marshmallows on cookie sheet or jelly roll pan; freeze 15 minutes.

▶ Microwave chocolate chips on HIGH 2½ minutes or until smooth, stirring every minute.

▶ Using skewer or fondue fork, dip each frozen marshmallow into melted chocolate until marshmallow is completely coated.

▶ Roll in coconut or decorative candies.

▶ Use another fork or metal spatula to place marshmallow onto waxed paper-lined cookie sheet or jelly roll pan.

▶ Chill or keep in cool dry place.   Approximately 38 to 40

Marshmallow Truffles

Neat Sweet Treats

Crispy, crunchy, sweet and chewy describe these fast-to-fix treats. Enlist the kids' help. They'll enjoy the making as much as the munching.

Caramelcorn

Helpful Hints

✓ Microwave popcorn makes *Caramelcorn* extra easy.

✓ Store popcorn snacks at room temperature in cookie tin or plastic container with tight-fitting lid.

✓ Use nonstick cooking spray to lightly grease pan for *Marshmallow Crispy Treats* and *Lemon Nut Bars*.

✓ To soften cream cheese quickly, unwrap 8 ounce package and place on microwave-safe plate. Microwave on MEDIUM (50%) 30 seconds.

Caramelcorn (opposite)

Prep time: 10 minutes
Microwave cooking time: 3 minutes
Conventional cooking time: 25 minutes

28   KRAFT Caramels
2   tablespoons cold water
2 1/2 qts. popped corn

▶ Preheat oven to 250°.

▶ Microwave caramels with water in 2-cup measure or medium bowl on HIGH 1½ minutes; stir.

▶ Continue microwaving on HIGH 30 seconds to 1 minute or until sauce is smooth, stirring every 30 seconds.

▶ Pour immediately over popped corn; toss until well coated. Spread onto greased cookie sheet to form single layer.

▶ Bake 20 to 25 minutes; break apart.   2½ quarts

Conventional:

▶ Melt caramels with water in saucepan over low heat, stirring until smooth. Continue as directed.

Marshmallow Crispy Treats

Prep/cooking time: 10 minutes
Microwave cooking time: 3 minutes

1/4   cup PARKAY Margarine
1   (10 1/2 oz.) bag (6 cups) KRAFT Miniature Marshmallows or 1 (10 oz.) bag KRAFT Jet-Puffed Marshmallows (40 marshmallows)
6   cups crisp rice cereal

▶ Melt margarine in 3-quart saucepan over low heat.

▶ Add marshmallows; stir until melted and well blended. Remove from heat.

▶ Stir in cereal until well coated; press into greased 13 x 9-inch baking pan. Cool. Cut into bars.   Approximately 2 dozen

Microwave:

▶ Microwave margarine in large bowl on HIGH 45 seconds or until melted.

▶ Add marshmallows; toss to coat with margarine.

▶ Microwave on HIGH 1½ minutes or until smooth when stirred, stirring after 45 seconds.

▶ Immediately stir in cereal until well coated; press into greased 13 x 9-inch baking pan. Cool. Cut into bars.

Lemon Nut Bars (below)

Prep time: 30 minutes
Cooking time: 25 minutes

1 1/3 cups flour
1/2   cup packed brown sugar
1/4   cup granulated sugar
3/4   cup PARKAY Margarine
1   cup old fashioned or quick oats, uncooked
1/2   cup chopped nuts
1   (8 oz.) pkg. PHILADELPHIA BRAND Cream Cheese, softened
1   egg
3   tablespoons lemon juice
1   tablespoon grated lemon peel

▶ Preheat oven to 350°.

▶ Stir together flour and sugars; cut in margarine until mixture resembles coarse crumbs. Stir in oats and nuts. Reserve 1 cup.

▶ Press remaining crumb mixture onto bottom of greased 13 x 9-inch baking pan. Bake 15 minutes.

▶ Beat cream cheese, egg, juice and peel in small mixing bowl at medium speed with electric mixer until well blended. Pour over crust; sprinkle with reserved crumb mixture.

▶ Bake 25 minutes. Cool. Cut into bars.
Approximately 3 dozen

Lemon Nut Bars

◄ Problem:

Surprise! When friends drop by unexpectedly, there's never a chip or pretzel to be found. Help!

▲ Solution:

Anytime can be party time when you have a collection of quick-fix appetizers and snacks at your fingertips. All these great ideas use on-hand ingredients and take only minutes to make.

Spur

Of The

Moment

Anytime can be party
time when you have a
collection of quick-fix
appetizers and snacks at
your fingertips. All these
great ideas use on-hand
ingredients and take
minutes to make.

Savory Snacks and Appetizers

Here's a snack for every taste. The *Classic Cheese Tray* is substantial enough to fill-in for a meal with the addition of fruit. *Seasoned Parmesan Popcorn* won't spoil the kids' appetites for dinner.

Classic Cheese Tray

Classic Cheese Tray (opposite)

Prep time: 10 minutes

1   (8 oz.) pkg. *100% Natural KRAFT Sharp Cheddar Cheese,* cubed
1   (8 oz.) pkg. *CASINO Natural Swiss Cheese,* sliced
      OSCAR MAYER Boiled Ham Slices
      OSCAR MAYER Salami Slices
      Celery sticks
      Tomato slices
      Cucumber slices

▶ Arrange ingredients on serving tray.

Quick Seafood Appetizer

Prep time: 5 minutes

¼   cup *SAUCEWORKS Cocktail Sauce*
1   (8 oz.) pkg. *PHILADELPHIA BRAND Cream Cheese*
1   (8 oz.) pkg. *LOUIS KEMP Crab Delights Flakes* or (6 oz.) pkg. frozen cooked tiny shrimp, thawed, drained

▶ Pour cocktail sauce over cream cheese; top with crab-flavored surimi seafood. Serve with crackers or party rye bread slices. Approximately 6 to 8 servings

Variations: Substitute any of the following for cocktail sauce and shrimp:

   OSCAR MAYER Bacon Slices, crisply cooked, crumbled and green onion slices.
   ⅓ cup chutney and 2 tablespoons chopped peanuts.
   ¼ cup jalapeño pepper jelly.
   ¼ cup salsa and *100% Natural KRAFT Shredded Mild Cheddar Cheese.*

Cheese and Bacon Spread

Prep time: 10 minutes
Microwave cooking time: 4 minutes

1   (8 oz.) pkg. *PHILADELPHIA BRAND Cream Cheese*
½   cup *MIRACLE WHIP Salad Dressing*
1   cup (4 ozs.) *100% Natural KRAFT Shredded Mild Cheddar Cheese*
2   tablespoons green onion slices

8   *OSCAR MAYER Bacon Slices,* crisply cooked, crumbled
½   cup crushed buttery crackers

▶ Microwave cream cheese on MEDIUM (50%) 30 seconds.
▶ Mix together cream cheese, salad dressing, cheddar cheese and onions until well blended.
▶ Spoon into 9-inch pie plate.
▶ Microwave on HIGH 4 minutes or until thoroughly heated, turning dish every 2 minutes. Sprinkle with combined bacon and cracker crumbs. Serve with assorted crackers. 2 cups

Seasoned Parmesan Popcorn (below)

Prep time: 5 minutes

¼   cup *PARKAY Margarine,* melted
1½   teaspoons Mexican seasoning
2   qts. popped corn
½   cup (2 ozs.) *KRAFT 100% Grated Parmesan Cheese*

▶ Mix together margarine and seasoning. Drizzle over popcorn; toss until well coated.
▶ Add cheese; toss to coat evenly. 2 quarts

Variation: Substitute 1 teaspoon coarse ground pepper and ½ teaspoon garlic powder for Mexican seasoning.

Seasoned Parmesan Popcorn

Savory Snacks and Appetizers
(continued)

Quesadillas

Quesadillas (opposite)

Prep time: 5 minutes
Microwave cooking time: 2 minutes

1   (6-inch) flour tortilla
⅓   cup (1⅓ ozs.) shredded *100% Natural KRAFT Cheddar or Monterey Jack Cheese*
1   tablespoon chopped green chilies, drained

▶ Place tortilla on paper towel-lined plate. Sprinkle with cheese and chilies.

▶ Microwave on MEDIUM (50%) 1 to 2 minutes or until cheese is melted.

▶ Fold tortilla in half. Serve with salsa, if desired.   1 serving

Variation: Substitute green onion slices, chopped tomatoes or pitted ripe olive slices for green chilies.

Cheesy Bread Appetizers

Prep time: 10 minutes
Cooking time: 7 minutes

1   cup (4 ozs.) *VELVEETA Shredded Pasteurized Process Cheese Food*
⅓   cup *KRAFT Real Mayonnaise*
¼   cup chopped green onions
4   *OSCAR MAYER Bacon Slices,* crisply cooked, crumbled
18   party rye bread slices, toasted

▶ Preheat oven to 350°.

▶ Mix together all ingredients except bread slices until well blended.

▶ Spread bread slices with cheese mixture.

▶ Bake 5 to 7 minutes, or until process cheese food is melted. 8 to 10 servings

Hot & Spicy Artichoke Spread

Prep time: 10 minutes
Microwave cooking time: 9 minutes

1   cup *KRAFT Real Mayonnaise* or *MIRACLE WHIP Salad Dressing*
1   cup (4 ozs.) *KRAFT 100% Grated Parmesan Cheese*
1   (14 oz.) can artichoke hearts, drained, chopped
1   (4 oz.) can chopped green chilies, drained

1   garlic clove, minced
2   tablespoons green onion slices
2   tablespoons chopped tomatoes

▶ Mix together all ingredients except onions and tomatoes; spoon into 9-inch pie plate or quiche dish.

▶ Microwave on MEDIUM (50%) 7 to 9 minutes or until mixture is thoroughly heated, stirring every 4 minutes.

▶ Stir before serving. Sprinkle with onions and tomatoes. Serve with crackers or pita bread wedges.   2 cups

Quick 'N Cheesy Nachos (below)

Prep time: 10 minutes

1   (8 oz.) pkg. tortilla chips
1   (8 oz.) jar *CHEEZ WHIZ Pasteurized Process Cheese Spread*
     Chopped tomatoes
     Green onion slices
     Pitted ripe olive slices
     Chopped green chilies

▶ Place chips on serving platter. Microwave process cheese spread according to label directions; pour over chips. Top with remaining ingredients.   4 to 6 servings

Variation: Substitute *CHEEZ WHIZ Pasteurized Process Cheese Spread with Jalapeño Peppers* or *CHEEZ WHIZ Mexican Pasteurized Process Cheese Spread* for process cheese spread.

Quick 'N Cheesy Nachos

Dips–In A Hurry

Dips are BIG again, offering convenience and a flavor to please everyone. These sweet and savory dips can be made in 15 minutes or less.

New Ranch Dip

Helpful Hints

✓ Keep a variety of dippers on hand – assorted crackers, breadsticks, pita chips, bagel chips, tortilla chips, pretzels.

✓ Fresh or canned fruit, frozen pound cake and marshmallows make tasty sweet dippers.

✓ Line a basket or tray with a thick layer of parsley or other greens. Arrange raw vegetable dippers on top.

✓ To keep fresh fruit dippers – apples, peaches, bananas and pears – from darkening, dip in orange or lemon juice.

✓ Add pizazz with an assortment of unusual bowls. Or, remove the top and center of a round loaf of French, sourdough or dark rye bread. Spoon the dip into the "bowl"; cut the interior bread into cubes and use as dippers.

New Ranch Dip (opposite)

Prep time: 10 minutes plus chilling

1	**cup sour cream**
1/2	**cup SEVEN SEAS VIVA RANCH! Dressing**
1/4	**cup (1 oz.) KRAFT 100% Grated Parmesan Cheese**
4	**OSCAR MAYER Bacon Slices, crisply cooked, crumbled**
2	**tablespoons green onion slices**

▶ Mix together ingredients until well blended; chill. Serve with vegetable dippers or crackers. 1½ cups

Variation: Substitute *RANCHER'S CHOICE Creamy Dressing* for ranch dressing.

Easy Cheesy Dip

Prep time: 5 minutes plus chilling
Microwave cooking time: 3 minutes

1	**(8 oz.) jar CHEEZ WHIZ Pasteurized Process Cheese Spread**
1	**(8 oz.) pkg. PHILADELPHIA BRAND Cream Cheese**
1/4	**cup chunky salsa**

▶ **Cold Method:** Beat ingredients at medium speed with electric mixer until well blended; chill. Serve with assorted crackers. 2 cups

▶ **Hot Method:** Microwave ingredients in 1-quart bowl on HIGH 3 minutes or until thoroughly heated, stirring every minute. Serve with tortilla chips. 2 cups

Variation: Substitute ⅓ cup chopped green onions for salsa.

Creamy Herb Dip

Prep time: 5 minutes
Cooking time: 5 minutes

2	**tablespoons chopped green onion**
1	**tablespoon PARKAY Margarine**
1	**(8 oz.) container PHILADELPHIA BRAND Soft Cream Cheese with Herb & Garlic**
1/4	**cup milk**
2	**tablespoons dry white wine**

▶ Saute onions in margarine in medium saucepan until tender.
▶ Stir in cream cheese, milk and wine; cook until cream cheese is melted. Serve warm with sourdough bread cubes. 1¼ cups

VELVEETA® Salsa Dip (below)

Cheese Spread

Prep time: 5 minutes
Microwave cooking time: 5 minutes
Cooking time: 10 minutes

1	**lb. VELVEETA Pasteurized Process Cheese Spread, cubed**
1	**(8 oz.) jar salsa or 1 (10 oz.) can diced tomatoes and green chilies, drained**
2	**tablespoons chopped cilantro (optional)**

▶ Microwave process cheese spread and salsa in 1½-quart bowl on HIGH 5 minutes or until thoroughly heated, stirring after 3 minutes.
▶ Add cilantro. Serve hot with tortilla chips and broiled red, green or yellow pepper wedges, if desired. 3 cups

Conventional :

▶ Stir process cheese spread and salsa over low heat until smooth.
▶ Add cilantro. Serve hot with tortilla chips or broiled red, green or yellow pepper wedges, if desired.

Variation: Substitute *VELVEETA Mexican Pasteurized Process Cheese Spread with Jalapeño Pepper* for process cheese spread and one (14 ½ oz.) can tomatoes, drained, cut up, for salsa.

VELVEETA® Salsa Dip
Cheese Spread

Dips–In A Hurry
(continued)

Creamy Caramel Dip

Creamy Caramel Dip (opposite)

Prep time: 10 minutes
Microwave cooking time: 5 minutes

1	(14 oz.) bag *KRAFT Caramels*
²/₃	cup half and half

▶ Microwave caramels with half and half in 1-quart bowl on HIGH 4 to 5 minutes or until dip is smooth, stirring every minute.

▶ Serve warm or at room temperature with fruit, pound cake or angel food cake cubes.   1¾ cups

Variation: Add 2 tablespoons almond, coffee or Irish cream flavored liqueur.

Mallow Fruit Dip

Prep time: 15 minutes

1	(8 oz.) pkg. *PHILADELPHIA BRAND Cream Cheese,* softened
1	(7 oz.) jar *KRAFT Marshmallow Creme*
1	tablespoon orange juice
1	teaspoon grated orange peel
	Dash of ground ginger (optional)

▶ Beat ingredients at medium speed with electric mixer until well blended. Serve with fruit.   1½ cups

Pizza Dip

Prep/microwave cooking time: 3 minutes

1	(8 oz.) jar *CHEEZ WHIZ Pasteurized Process Cheese Spread*
1	(8 oz.) can pizza sauce

▶ Heat process cheese spread according to package directions.

▶ Mix together process cheese spread and pizza sauce.

▶ Microwave on HIGH 1 to 1½ minutes or until thoroughly heated, stirring after 1 minute. Serve with breadsticks or vegetable dippers, if desired.   1¾ cups

Garlic Cheese Dip

Prep time: 10 minutes plus chilling

1	cup *MIRACLE WHIP Salad Dressing*
1	cup (4 ozs.) *100% Natural KRAFT Shredded Sharp Cheddar Cheese*
1	cup sour cream
½	cup (2 ozs.) *KRAFT 100% Grated Parmesan Cheese*
½	cup green onion slices or finely chopped white onion
½	teaspoon garlic powder

▶ Mix together ingredients until well blended; chill. Serve with assorted crackers.   3 cups

Spinach-Parmesan Dip (below)

Prep time: 10 minutes plus chilling

1	(10 oz.) pkg. *BIRDS EYE Chopped Spinach,* thawed, well drained
1	cup *MIRACLE WHIP Salad Dressing*
1	cup sour cream
½	cup (2 ozs.) *KRAFT 100% Grated Parmesan Cheese*
1	(8 oz.) can water chestnuts, drained, chopped
⅛	teaspoon ground red pepper

▶ Mix together ingredients until well blended; chill. Serve with assorted crackers.   4 cups

Spinach-Parmesan Dip

◀ Problem:

What's for dinner? Fast food in front of the television–again. I need ideas for turning the dinner hour into a family hour.

▲ Solution:

The easy recipes, serving suggestions and helpful hints in this book are the ticket to sharing a well-balanced meal.

D

E

Weeknight Menu:

Monday

Tuesday

Wednesday

Thursday

Friday

Notes:

Notes: